MW00929182

CRASH COURSE: CHINESE

LEARN PRACTICAL, EVERYDAY CHINESE FAST WITH A NATIVE SPEAKER

Polyglot Language Guides
Celine Li

Copyright © 2015 Polyglot Language Guides

All Rights Reserved. No part of this publication may be reproduced, stored in a retrieval system, or transmitted in any form or by any means, electronic, mechanical, recording, or otherwise, without the prior written consent of the author.

TABLE OF CONTENTS

A Snippet of What You Will Get

1. Over 500 Everyday Conversational Phrases Organized by Topic:

for a list of conversational topics, see the table of contents

I'm hungry   *wǒ è le*   我饿了

Let's go eat   *wǒmen qù chīfàn ba*   我们去吃饭吧

Do you have vegetarian dishes?   *nǐmen yǒu sù shí ma?*
你们有素食吗?

I'm allergic to … *wǒ dùi* (insert allergen name) *guòmǐn*   我
对___过敏

    eggs   *jīdàn*   鸡蛋

    fish   *yú*   鱼

    dairy   *nǎi lèi*   奶类

    nuts   *jiān guǒ*   坚果

2. Commonly Used Vocabulary Lists:

beautiful   *měi lì*   美丽

handsome   *shuài*   帅

fun   *hǎowán*   好玩

interesting   *yǒuqù*   有趣

boring   *wúliáo*   无聊

3. COLLOQUIAL CHINESE DISTINCTIONS:

excuse me (coming through)

jièguò   借过

láojià   劳驾   (used in Mainland China, informal)

4. FOUNDATIONAL GRAMMAR POINTS:

Negating Verbs

On its own, [bù 不] means 'no.' But, when placed directly before a verb, preposition, or adverb, [bù 不] works as a negating element. [bù 不] is used to negate both one-time actions and habitual actions.

Note, however, [bù 不] cannot be used in conjunction with [yǒu 有 'to have'] as a negating element. The negated form of [yǒu 有] is [méiyǒu 没有 'does not have']. On its own, [méi 没] means 'none.'

Examples:

<u>Negating a Single Action</u>

She is not eating dinner tonight
tā jīnwǎn bù chīfàn
她今晚**不吃**饭
(tā = she, jīnwǎn = tonight, bù = not, chīfàn = eat)

End of Snippet

—

The Forbidden City (Zǐ Jìn Chéng 紫禁城), Beijing

Introduction

Learn 80% of Everyday Chinese with This Book

Have you ever heard of the 80/20 Rule? Also known as Pareto's Principle, the 80/20 rule provides that 80% of the results are achieved by 20% of the total action. This rule applies to nearly every aspect of life, including learning languages. In essence, 20% of a language is what's actually used 80% of the times. This 20% of golden material consists of the most common words and phrases used in daily situations. If you knew this 20% of material, you'd be able to understand 80% of a given language, in its everyday use. And this is exactly what this book aims to do—provide you with that essential 20% of the Chinese language that is used 80% of the times.

The Most Spoken Language in the World

Chinese is the most commonly spoken language in the world. Nearly 1.2 billion people, or 1/6 of the world's population, speak some form of Chinese as their first language. The majority of Chinese speakers speak Mandarin, or Putonghua, which is this book's focus. Today's standard Chinese is based on the form of Mandarin spoken in China's capital, Beijing. The author of this book is a native Chinese-speaker who grew up in Beijing and has traveled throughout China.

How to Use This Book

If you are going to China tomorrow and just need the basics, skim Chapter 1 for a guide to pronunciation and head to Chapter 3 for the most essential survival phrases. Then, go to Chapter 5 for situation-specific phrases and Chapter 6 for a list of the most useful Chinese characters to recognize. If you have a bit more time, I recommend fully understanding the grammar foundations in Chapter 2.

Chapter 1: Pronunciation Made Easy

Thanks to the Romanization system, Hanyu Pinyin, which uses the roman alphabet system familiar to English speakers, Chinese pronunciation is easy to learn and follows predictable patterns. To pronounce a word in Chinese, there are 3 key components: the tone, the initial sound (consonant) and the final sound (vowel or vowel combination) to note. This chapter will introduce you to the Chinese alphabet and provide you with what you need to know to pronounce virtually every word in Mandarin Chinese.

Hanyu Pinyin [hànyǔ pīnyīn 汉语拼音], or 'pinyin' for short, is a phonetic system developed in the 1950s to transcribe the Mandarin pronunciations of Chinese characters to the Latin alphabet. Hànyǔ literally means "Chinese language" and Pīnyīn means "joint sounds."

The Tones

In standard Mandarin Chinese, there are four primary tones and a neutral tone.

The **first tone** (high-level tone) is a high and steady sound. Imagine an opera singer voicing "laaa laaa laaa." The "aaa" is a very flat sound.

The **second tone** (rising tone) rises from a middle pitch to a high pitch. This can be likened to someone asking "huh?" or "what?" in an inquisitive way.

The **third tone** (dipping tone) starts with a middle pitch and drops to a mid-low pitch. Then, it quickly rises at the end. To sound this tone accurately, you should really feel your tongue at work.

The **fourth tone** (falling tone) starts at a high pitch and then falls to low.

The **neutral tone** can be described as lacking a tone. It is short and light. Sounding this tone can be likened to saying something with an exclamation mark at the end.

To hear the tones pronounced, visit (https://chinese.yabla.com/chinese-pinyin-chart.php)

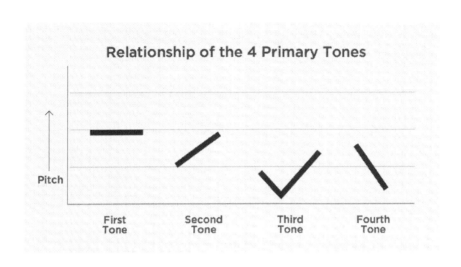

Relationship of the 4 Primary Tones

Tone	First	Second	Third	Fourth	Fifth
Pinyin	*ā*	*á*	*ǎ*	*à*	*a*
Description	High	Rising	Low or dipping	Falling	Neutral, light
Example	mā	má	mǎ	mà	ma

Consonants

There are 20 consonants in Chinese and they form 23 **initial sounds**. Out of these 23 sounds, there are three combination sounds- ch, sh, zh. Most of Chinese consonants are pronounced similarly to the way that they are pronounced in English. The exceptions are c, q, r, x, and zh.

List of Chinese Initial Sounds in Proper Order
b p m f
d t n l
g k h
j q x
z c s r
zh ch sh
y w

Initial Sounds: Exactly Like English

f   **f**ather

l   **l**ove

m   **m**om

n   **n**o

s   **s**ing

sh   **sh**ip, **sh**ank

w   **w**ay

y   **y**es

Initial Sounds: Slightly Different from English
This list is, for the most part, similar to their English counterparts. Pay attention to the nuanced differences.

b　bud, bubble

ch　chap, ditch

d　cig, mad

g　goat, cigar

h　hen, haha

j　genie, jeep

k　ken

p　pop

t　tip

z　zen, zest

Initial Sounds: Tricky and Really Different From English
Pay close attention to this list.

c　tsar (cong = ts-ong)

q　cheese, cheat (qin = chin)

r　rut, ruth (re = r'ugh)

x　sheep (xi = shee)

zh　gem, job, jack (zhang = jahng)

Compound Finals	Nasal Ending Finals

ai	an ⁓	ang
eye, b**ye**	**an**	**ahng, h**u**ng**
ao	en	eng
h**ow**	h**en**	**uhng**
ei	ian	iang
h**ey**	kardash**ian**	**eon**
ia	in	ing
-ya, ma**ya**	**in**	**-ying**, sa**ying**
iao	uan	iong
-yao (ee-auw)	**woo-an**	**ee-own**
ie	üan	ong
ee-yeh	**yoo-an**	**ohng**
iou	uen	uang
ee-owe	**woo-en**	**woo-ahng**
ou	ün	ueng
owe	**yoon**	**woo-ehng**
ua		
wooah		
uai		
wooeye		
üe		
yoo-eh		
uei		
woo-aey		
uo		

15

woo-woh		

Vowels

In Mandarin Chinese there are 6 simple vowels: a, e, i, o, u, ü. These simple vowels combine to form 13 compound finals (ai, ao, ei, ia, iao, ie, iou, ou, ua, uai, üe, uei, uo) and 16 nasal finals (an, en, ian, in, uan, üan, uen, ün, ang, eng, iang, ing, iong, ong, uang, ueng).

Simple Vowels

a   father

e   sound in between "**eh**" and "**uh**"

i   **is**, w**e**

o   **aw**, **a**ll, w**oe**

u   w**oo**, s**ou**p

ü   **yooo**

Chapter 2: Foundational Grammar

Chinese grammar is easier than you think. Compared to languages such as English, German, and the Romantic languages, Chinese grammar is a piece of a cake. Nouns don't have genders. There's no need to conjugate verbs and there are no irregular verb or nouns. For the most part, the grammar doesn't change depending on the speaker's gender. Overall, the Chinese language is logical, consistent, and follows patterns.

Sentence Structure

3 Key Points About Chinese Sentence Structure

First, the basic word order in Chinese is generally **Subject-Verb-Object**. Modifiers precede the words that they describe.

Examples.

She drinks water   tā hē shuǐ
她喝水 (tā = she, hē = drink(s), shuǐ = water)

I like American music   wǒ xǐhuān meǐguó yīnyuè
我喜欢美国音乐 (wǒ = I, xǐhuān = like(s), měiguó = American, yīnyuè = music)

Second, most European languages are subject-prominent but the Chinese language is **topic-prominent**. This simply means that the topic of the sentence plays a key role in defining the sentence formation.

Examples.

I take a walk in the park every morning   wǒ měitiān zǎoshàng zài gōngyuán sànbù
我每天早上在公园散步 (wǒ = I, měitiān = everyday, zǎoshàng = morning, zài = at, gōngyuán = park, sànbù = walk)

Note: Here, the topic revolves around walking in "the park." Thus, the topic shapes the sentence formation and takes precedence over the verb.

Third and last, Chinese, to an extent can be considered a **null-subject** language. This means that the subject may be omitted if it can be inferred from the specific context.

Example.

I didn't see it   méiyǒu kàndào
没有看到 (méiyǒu = did not, kàndào = see)

Note: The subject here is omitted and depending on the context, it could be one of many pronouns, such as I, we, you, he, she, it…

When someone asks you "how are you doing" in Chinese, it's perfectly grammatically correct to say "I'm okay" without the "I."

I'm okay háihǎo
还好 (hái = still, hǎo = good)

Nouns and Plurals

Nouns

Nouns [míngcí 名词] in Chinese, for the most part, function just as they do in English. Take note of how plurals are constructed and how classifiers are used.

Plurals

Chinese nouns don't change when referred to in the plural. In most cases involving people, [men 们] is used as a plural marker. Another way to indicate plurality in Chinese is using demonstrative pronouns [zhè 这 'this'／nà 那 'that'] with the plural indicator [xiē 些].

these zhèxiē 这些

those nàxiē 那些

Examples.

people rénmen
人们 (rén = person, men = plural indicator)

We / Us wǒmen
我们 (wǒ = I/me, men = plural indicator)

These countries zhèxiē guójiā
这些国家 (zhèxiē = these, guójiā* = country)
Note here, the noun, 'country (guójiā)' is singular and will never change its form even when it's plural noun. All nouns in Chinese behave in this manner.

Pronouns

Chinese pronouns are fairly simple. There's no written or pronunciation differentiation between subject pronouns and object pronouns. To create the possessive pronoun state, simply add [de 的] after the corresponding personal pronoun. To create the corresponding plural state of a personal pronoun, simply add [men 们] after it.

Formal vs. Informal You

Much like the 'Tu' and 'Usted' in Spanish, Chinese distinguishes between a formal and informal 'You.' Both [nín 您] and [nǐ 你] mean 'You.' When speaking to elders, someone whom you respect, or your boss, use [nín 您] to be polite. When speaking to familiar people, friends, or those who are younger, use [nǐ 你] .

	Subject / Object Pronouns	
Singular	**I/ me**	wǒ 我
	you (familiar)	nǐ 你
	you (formal)	nín 您
	he/ him	tā 他
	she/ her	tā 她
	it	tā 它
Plural	**we/us**	wǒmen 我们
	you (familiar)	nǐmen 你们
	you (formal)	nínmen 您们
	they/ them	tāmen 他们 (masculine, also used for

		mixed gender groups)
		tāmen 她们 (feminine)
		tāmen 它们 (neutral)

	Possessive Pronouns	
Singular	**my/mine**	*wǒ de* 我的
	your/yours (familiar)	*nǐ de* 你的
	your/yours (formal)	*nín de* 您的
	his	*tā de* 他的
	her/hers	*tā de* 她的
	its	*tā de* 它的
Plural	**our/ours**	*wǒmen de* 我们的
	your/yours (familiar)	*nǐmen de* 你们的
	your/yours (formal)	*nǐmen de* 您们的
	their/theirs	*tāmen de* 他们 (masculine, also used for mixed gender groups) *tāmen de* 她们 (feminine)

		tāmen de 它们 (neutral)

	Reflexive Pronouns	
Singular	**myself**	*wǒ zìjǐ* 我自己
	yourself (familiar)	*nǐ zìjǐ* 你自己
	yourself (formal)	*nín zìjǐ* 您自己
	himself	*tā zìjǐ* 他自己
	herself	*tā zìjǐ* 她自己
	itself	*tā zìjǐ* 它自己
Plural	**ourself/ ourselves**	*wǒmen zìjǐ* 我们自己
	yourself (familiar)/ **yourselves**	*nǐmen zìjǐ* 你们自己
	yourself (formal)/ **yourselves**	*nínmen zìjǐ* 您们自己
	themselves	*tāmen zìjǐ* 他们自己 (masculine, also used for mixed gender groups) *tāmen zìjǐ* 她们自己 (feminine)

		tāmen zìjǐ 它们自己 (neutral)

Demonstrative Pronouns	
this	*zhège* 这个
that	*nàge* 那个
these	*zhèxiē* 这些
those	*nàxiē* 那些

Objects

Like in English, both the direct object and indirect object usually follows the verb

The direct object usually follows the **Subject + Verb + Object** structure.

Examples.

I'm American   *wǒ shì měiguó rén*

我是美国人   (wǒ = I, shì* = am, měiguó = U.S.A., rén = person)

*Note: In Chinese there is no such thing as verb conjugation. Thus, all forms of "to be" are the same, that is, 'shì.'

She is my mother *tā shì wǒ de māma*
她是我的妈妈 (tā = she, shì = is, wǒde = my, māma = mom)

When a verb takes both an indirect object and a direct object, the indirect object usually precedes the direct one.

Example.

I gave him a cookie *wǒ gěile tā yígè bǐnggān*
我给了他一个饼干 (wǒ = I, gěile = gave, tā (indirect obj.) = him, yígè = one, bǐnggān = cookie (direct obj.))

Adjectives

In Chinese, adjectives can be used in two ways, either **attributively**, such as before a noun, or **predicatively**, where they behave more like verbs.

Attributive Adjectives

In this use case, the connector [de 的] is often added after the adjective. However, this is not always necessary. Attributive adjectives are always placed before the nouns that they modify.

Examples.

expensive   *guì de*   贵的

expensive car   *guì de chē*   贵的车

expensive purse   *guì de píbāo*   贵的皮包

beautiful   *měilì de*   美丽的

beautiful flower   *měilì de huā*   美丽的花

Attributive adjectives can also be used to **indicate possession**. The construction pattern is parallel to the examples above. The connector [de 的] follows a noun or pronoun to attribute possession to that noun or pronoun. Let's look at some examples.

Examples.

mom's   *māma de*   妈妈的

mom's book   *māma de shū*   妈妈的书

his   *tā de*   他的

his suggestion   *tā de jiànyì*   他的建议

Predicative Adjectives

Predicative adjectives link to the noun they modify through a verb. When used predicatively, the adjective is often preceded by [shì 是 'to be'] or [hěn 很 'very']. The predicative adjective follows the subject that they modify.

Examples.

It's pretty   *tā hěn piàoliang*
它很漂亮   (tā = it, hěn = very, piàoliang = pretty)
Note that the predicative adjective 'piàoliang' follows the subject it modifies, 'tā.'

It's really pretty   *tā zhēn piàoliang*
它真漂亮   (tā = it, zhēn = really, piàoliang = pretty)

Showing Gradation

To show the intensity or extremity of an adjective, add [jí le 级 了 'extremely'] after an adjective.

Examples.

extremely pretty   漂亮极了   *piàoliang jíle*
extremely good (**great**)   *hǎo jíle*   好极了

Common Adjectives

beautiful *měi lì* 美丽

handsome *shuài* 帅

fun *hǎowán* 好玩

interesting *yǒuqù* 有趣

boring *wúliáo* 无聊

funny (when something is funny) *hǎoxiào* 好笑

old *jiù* 旧

young *niánqīng* 年轻

new *xīn* 新

important *zhòngyào* 重要

difficult *nán* 难

easy *jiǎndān* 简单

spicy *là* 辣

sweet *tián* 甜

tall *gāo* 高

short (height) *ǎi* 矮

short (length) *duǎn* 短

bad /evil *huài* 坏

good *hǎo* 好

Adverbs

Chinese adverbs function essentially the same way as adverbs do in English. Adverbs usually come before the verb but after the subject of the verb.

<u>Common adverbs</u>:

temporal adverbs

yesterday   *zuótiān*   昨天

today   *jīntiān*   今天

tomorrow   *míngtiān*   明天

now   *xiànzài*   现在

then   *ránhòu*   然后

later   *hòulái*   后来

tonight   *jīnwǎn*   今晚

immediately   *mǎshàng*   马上

already   *yǐjīng*   已经

recently   *zuìjìn*   最近

soon   *bùjiǔ*   不久

still   *réng*   仍

adverbs of place

here   *zhèlǐ*   这里

there   *nàlǐ*   那里

everywhere   *dàochù*   到处

nowhere   *wúchù*   无处

adverbs of manner

very   *hěn*   很   (Note: in Chinese, "very" functions much like a verb)

quite   *xiāngdāng*   相当

really   *zhēnde*   真地

almost   *jīhū*   几乎

absolutely   *juéduì*   绝对

together   *yīqǐ*   一起

adverbs of frequency

always   *zǒngshì*   总是

usually   *tōngcháng*   通常

sometimes   *yǒushí*   有时

occasionally   *ǒuěr*   偶尔

rarely   *hěnshǎo*   很少

never   *cóngbù*   从不

Verbs

In Chinese, verbs do not have tenses and thus never change forms. Luckily, you don't have to worry about verb conjugation, irregular verbs, or subject-verb agreement. To indicate past, present, or future actions, different time phrases are used in conjunction with the verb.

Past Tense

To indicate past tense, the special particle [le 了] and word [guò 过 'pass/ past'] are commonly used. Often, [le 了] is added at the end of a sentence or after a verb phrase to signify the action in the sentence has been completed. To specify the past action was completed in a certain time, add the time indicator (i.e. yesterday, last month) at the beginning of the sentence after the pronoun.

Examples.

I don't love you anymore   *wǒ bú ài nǐ le*

我不爱你了 (wǒ = I, bú = not, ài = love, nǐ = you, le = past tense particle)

I understand now   *wǒ míngbái le*
我明白了 (wǒ = I, míngbái =understand, le = past tense particle)

I ate at the cafeteria yesterday   *wǒ zuótiān zài shítáng chīfàn le*
我昨天在食堂吃饭了 (wǒ = I, zuótiān = yesterday, zài = at, shítáng = cafeteria, chīfàn = eat, le = past tense particle)

When you've been to a place or have done an activity before, place [guò 过 'pass/ past'] after the verb to indicate the past tense.

Example.

I've been to London   *wǒ qùguò lúndūn*
我去过伦敦 (wǒ = I qù = go, guò = pass/ past, lúndūn = London)

Future Tense

To indicate the future tense, add the auxiliary verb [yào 要 'want'] or [huì 会 'will'] before the verb. [yào 要 'want'] indicates that one wants to do a certain action in the future.

[huì 会 'will'], on the other hand, indicates that one will do a certain action in the future.

Examples.

What do you want to buy?   *nǐ yào mǎi shénme dōngxī?*
你要买什么东西? (nǐ = you, yào = want, mǎi = buy, shénme = what, dōngxī = thing)

What will you buy?   *nǐ huì mǎi shénme dōngxī?*
你会买什么东西? (nǐ = you, huì = will, mǎi = buy, shénme = what, dōngxī = thing?

Verb Stacking

In Chinese, it's common for two verbs to be stacked together in usage. This often occurs through coverbs, auxiliary verbs, or verbal complements.

Coverbs

The Chinese language contains a class of words, known as coverbs, which are essentially a cross between verbs and prepositions. Not understanding the function of coverbs is a huge pitfall among new Chinese learners. Coverbs are derived from verbs but function more like prepositions in that they indicate some circumstances accompanying the main verb.

Unlike English prepositions, which usually follow the verb, Chinese coverbs always precede the verb.

Common Coverbs

Corresponding Preposition

to start from   *cóng* 从   (followed by place/time)

to be face to face with   *duì* 对   (followed by people/knowledge)

to give to   *gěi* 给   (followed by people/organization)

to go toward   *wǎng* 往   (followed by direction/place)

to use with   *yòng* 用   (followed by nouns)

to locate at/in/on   *zài* 在   (followed by location or time)

to sit/ to take (vehicle)   *zuò* 坐   (followed by vehicles of transportation)

Example.

I'll go from school to the theater (Also: I'm going from school to the theater)

wǒ cóng xuéxiào qù diànyǐngyuàn

我从学校去电影院   (wǒ = I, cóng = to start from, xuéxiào = school, qù = go, diànyǐngyuàn = movie theater)

Auxiliary Verbs

Just as in English, an auxiliary verb precedes a verb to "assist" the verb. Common Chinese auxiliary verbs are listed below.

Basic construction pattern: S + Auxiliary Verb + Main Verb + Object.

Common Auxiliary Verbs

Expressing capability

to be able to, to be capable of   *néng*   能
can, to be possible, to be able to, will   *huì*   会

Expressing possibility

may   *néng*   能
may   *kěyǐ*   可以
might (happen)   *kěnéng*   可能

Expressing necessity

should, ought to   *gāi*   该

should   *yào*   要

Expressing obligation

to have to, must   *děi*   得

Expressing willingness

to dare to   *gǎn*   敢

to want to, to think about doing   xiǎng   想

Examples.

She can speak Chinese   *tā huì shuō zhōngwén*
她会说中文   (tā = she, huì = can, shuō = speak, zhōngwén = Chinese)

We can help you   *wǒmen kěyǐ bāngzhù nǐ*
我们可以帮助你   (wǒmen = we, kěyǐ = can, bāngzhù = help, nǐ = you)

Conjunctions

Conjunctions in Chinese function as their English counterparts do- to connect things.

Common conjunctions

and   *hé*   和

or   *háishì*   还是 (used in questions)

or   huòzhě   或者 (used with words, phrases, and sentences)

if   *rúguǒ*   如果

yet   *búguò*   不过

so   *yīncǐ*   因此

but   *dànshì*   但是

because   *yīnwèi*   因为

therefore   *suǒyǐ*   所以

not only...but also   *búdàn... érqiě*   不但…而且

Examples.

you and I (me)... *nǐ hé wǒ*
你和我 (nǐ = you, hé = and, wǒ = I/me)

He and I work together *wǒ hé tā yīqǐ gōngzuò* 我和他一起工作

beer or wine? *píjiǔ háishì pútáojiǔ?* 啤酒还是葡萄酒?

Negation

Negating Verbs

On its own, [bù 不] means 'no.' But, when placed directly before a verb, preposition, or adverb, [bù 不] works as a negating element. [bù 不] is used to negate both one-time actions and habitual actions.

Note, however, [bù 不] cannot be used in conjunction with [yǒu 有 'to have') as a negating element. The negated form of [yǒu 有] is [méiyǒu 没有 'does not have']. On its own, [méi 没] means 'none.'

Examples.

Negating a Single Action

She is not eating dinner tonight *tā jīnwǎn bù chīfàn*
她今晚不吃饭 (tā = she, jīnwǎn = tonight, bù = not, chīfàn = eat)

Negating a Habitual Action

She does not drink alcohol   *tā bù hē jiǔ*

她不喝酒   (tā = she, bù = not, hē = drink, jiǔ = alcohol.)

Classifiers

A key distinction between Chinese and most Western languages is the necessity of classifiers. In Chinese and many East Asian languages, a numeral can never quantify a noun by itself. Thus, classifiers, or 'measure' words, are used in phrases in combination with a noun and a numeral. The classifier follows the numeral but precedes the noun. In English, classifiers are not uncommon. A spoonful of sugar, two stacks of paper, three dozen donuts… But in many cases, English does not require the use of classifiers. For instance, "two rabbits" in Chinese is something like this: two + classifier word for mammals + rabbits.

Note: The Chinese classifier, unlike its English counterpart, does not take a plural form when the numeral is plural.

Classifiers are also used with demonstratives, such as this and that. When a noun is modified by an adjective, the classifier precedes both the noun and the adjective.

Most Common Classifiers

a handful   *bǎ*   把   (used for long, flat objects and things with handles)

a volume of   *běn*   本   (used for books, printed materials)

a unit, part of   *bù*   部   (used for novels, movies, TV series)

portion of   *fèn*   份   (used for portions, batches and servings of food)

an item of   *gè*   个   (used for individual things, people — general, a catch-all measure word)

a mouth   *kǒu*   口   (used for things with mouths— people and some domestic animals)

piece of   *kuài*   块   (used for pieces/slices, including bricks and cake)

a surface   *miàn*   面   (used for flat and smooth objects, such as mirrors)

a row of   *pái*   排   (used for objects grouped in rows)

a pair   *shuāng*   双   (used for items that naturally come in pairs)

sheet of   *zhāng*   张   (used for flat objects or items with a flat surface, such as table and paper)

one *zhī* 只 (used for one of a pair and many animals)

type of *zhǒng* 种 (used for items that come in different breeds or types)

Examples.

Is this the last bus? *zhè shìbúshì zuì hòu yì bān chē?*
这是不是最后一**班**车? (zhè = this, shìbúshì = is it?, zuì hòu, last yì = 1, bān = classifier for car or vehicle, chē = car?)

three sisters *sān ge jiěmèi*
三个姐妹 (sān = 3, ge = catchall classifier, jiěmèi = sister(s))

Notes on the Chinese Language

<u>Homophones</u> – In Chinese, there are many words that sound exactly the same but have different meanings. Although their characters are written differently, it is still difficult to distinguish certain words from hearing them alone.

<u>Homographs</u> – There are a handful of words that have two pronunciations and different meanings and uses associated with each pronunciation. For example, an homograph in English is the word "bow," with could be used as bow and arrow or to bow down.

<u>Regional Dialects</u> – Each region of China, with the exception of Beijing, has its own dialect in addition to speaking Mandarin Chinese. The Mandarin spoken by different regions also have distinct regional accents. The Beijing version of Mandarin is known for having an "er" slur at the end of words. For example, in standard Mandarin, "no way" is *méimén*, but in the Beijing accent, it is *méimén'er*.

Chapter 3: Essential Survival Phrases

Pronouns Recap

Remember that pronouns don't change form in Chinese. For a refresher on pronouns, go to Chapter 2.

I/me   *wǒ*   我

you (singular familiar)   *nǐ*   你

she/her   *tā*   她

he/him   *tā*   他

it   *tā*   它

we/us   *wǒmen*   我们

you (plural familiar)   *nǐmen*   你们

they/them   *tāmen*   他们

Greetings

hello   *nǐ hǎo*   你好

How are you?   *nǐ hǎo ma?*   你好吗？

I'm great /I'm fine   *wǒ hěnhǎo*   我很好

I'm okay   *wǒ háihǎo*   我还好

good morning   *zǎo ān*   早安

good evening   *wǎnshàng hǎo*   晚上好

good night   *wǎn ān*   晚安

good afternoon   *xiàwǔ hǎo*   下午好

goodbye   *zàijiàn*   再见

bye bye   *bái bái*   拜拜

Basics

please   *qǐng*   请

thank you   *xièxiè*   谢谢

you're welcome   *bú kèqi*   不客气。

I'm sorry   *duìbùqǐ*   对不起

no problem / it's okay   *méi guānxi*   没关系

excuse me (asking for something)   *qǐng wèn*   请问

excuse me (coming through)   *jièguò*   借过

　láojià   劳驾 (Mainland China, informal)

excuse me (for disturbing…)   dǎrǎo le   打扰了

welcome (you)   *huānyíng nǐ*   欢迎你

Do you speak English? *nǐ huì shuō yīngyǔ ma?* 你会说英文吗

Is there someone here who speaks English? *zhèlǐ yǒu rén huì shuō yīngyǔ ma?* 这里有人会说英语吗?

please speak slowly *qǐng shuō màn yìdiǎn* 请说慢一点

please say it again *qǐng nǐ zài shuō yí biàn* 请你再说一遍

During Emergencies

help (in emergencies) *jiùmìng* 救命

please help me (assist me) *qǐng bāng wǒ* 请帮我

please help me call 911 (110) *qǐng bāng wǒ dǎ yāo yāo líng* 请帮我打 110

(In China, the number for the police is 110, for fire service is 119 and for an ambulance is 120. In Taiwan, the number for the police is 110 and for fire or an ambulance is 119.)

call (a/an/the)… *jiào* 叫

    doctor *yī shēng* 医生

    paramedics *jíjiù yuán* 急救员

    ambulance *jiùhù chē* 救护车

    police *jǐngchá* 警察

go to (the)… qù 去

> **police station** *jǐngchá jú* 警察局

> **hospital** *yī yuàn* 医院

> **emergency room** *jízhěn shì* 急诊室

fire station *xiāofáng shǔ* 消防署

nurse *hù shi* 护士

someone has fainted *yǒu rén yūndǎo le* 有人晕倒了

hurt/injured *shòushāng le* 受伤了

Is it serious? *yánzhòng ma?* 严重吗?

very serious *hěn yánzhòng* 很严重

not serious *bù yánzhòng* 不严重

robbery *qiǎngjié* 抢劫

thief *xiǎo tōu* 小偷

I've been robbed *wǒ bèi qiǎngjié le* 我被抢劫了

I lost my… *wǒ diū le wǒ de…* 我丢了我的…

> **wallet** *qiánbāo* 钱包

> **money** *qián* 钱

passport *hùzhào* 护照

purse *píbāo* 皮包

backpack *shūbāo* 书包

Asking Questions

who *shéi* 谁

when *shénme shíhòu* 什么时候

why *wèi shénme* 为什么

how *zěnyàng* 怎样

how much *duōshǎo* 多少

how many *jǐge* 几个

what *shénme* 什么?

where *nǎ lǐ* 哪里

Answering Questions

yes *shì* 是

no *búshì* 不是

maybe *kěnéng* 可能

probably dàgài 大概

I don't know   *wǒ bù zhīdào*   我不知道

I don't understand   *wǒ tīng bùdǒng*   我听不懂

General Question Construction in Chinese

Pronoun/Noun + Verb + (Object) + Question Word or
Question Particle

Examples.

Are you married?   *nǐ jiéhūn le ma*   你结婚了吗?
You + Have Married + Ma (Question Particle)
   Yes, I'm married   *wǒ jiéhūn le*   我结婚了

Where do you live/Where are you staying at?   *nǐ zhùzài*
nǎlǐ   你住在哪里?
You + Live at + Where (Question Word)
   I'm staying at the (Beijing) Hotel   *wǒ zhùzài*
(běijīng) jiǔdiàn   我住在(北京)酒店

What do you do? (for work)   *nǐ zuò shénme gōngzuò*   你
做什么工作?
You + Work + What (Question word)
   I'm a student. wǒ shi xuéshēng 我是学生

Asking for Necessities

Where is the restroom/toilet (please)? *(qǐngwèn) cèsuǒ zài nǎli?* (请问)厕所在哪里?

restroom (informal) *cèsuǒ* 厕所

restroom (more formal) *xǐshǒujiān* 洗手间

May I get on the Internet? *kěyǐ shàngwǎng ma?* 可以上网吗?

Is the Internet free? *shàngwǎng shì miǎnfèi de ma?* 上网是免费的吗?

May I have the password? *kěyǐ gěi wǒ mìmǎ ma?* 可以给我密码吗?

Are there outlets? *zhèlǐ yǒu diànyuán ma?* 这里有电源吗?

May I use your phone? *wǒ kěyǐ yòng nǐ de diànhuà ma?* 我可以用你的电话吗?

Is there a public phone? *zhèlǐ yǒu gōngyòng diànhuà ma?* 这里有公用电话吗?

Asking for Directions

how do I get to (the)… ?　*zěnme qù…*　怎么去…

 train station　*huǒchē zhàn*　火车站

 bus station　*gōngchē zhàn*　公车站

 subway station　*dì tiě zhàn*　地铁站

 airport?　*jī chǎng*　机场

 hotel?　(insert hotel name) *jiǔdiàn*　____酒店

How much is the ticket? (for vehicles)　*chēpiào duōshǎo qián*　车票多少钱?

Is it near?　*lí de jìn ma?*　离得近吗?

Is it far?　*lí de yuǎn ma?*　离得远吗?

Where can I find taxis?　*qǐngwèn zài nǎer kěyǐ zhǎodào chūzūchē?*　请问在哪里可以找到出租车?

street　*jiē*　街

very narrow street　*hútòng*　胡同

left　*zuǒbiān*　左边

right　*yòubiān*　右边

turn left　*xiàng zuǒ zhuǎn*　向左转

turn right　*xiàng yòu zhuǎn*　向右转

straight ahead　*wǎngqián zǒu*　往前走

go that way　*wǎng nèibiān zǒu*　往那边走

51

north   *běi*   北

south   *nán*   南

east   *dōng*   东

west   *xī*   西

I'm lost   *wǒ mílù le*   我迷路了

Do you have a map?   *nǐ yǒu dìtú ma?*   你有地图吗？

Where can I buy a map?   *wǒ zài nǎlǐ kěyǐ mǎi dìtú?*   我在哪里可以买地图？

On the Taxi

taxi   *chū zū chē*   出租车

please take me to…   *qǐng kāidào …*   请开到…

stop the car   *tíngchē*   停车

It's here   *dào le*   到了

It's across the street   *zài mǎlù dùi miàn*   在马路对面

make a U-turn   *diàotóu*   掉头

past the traffic light   *guò le hónglǜdēng*   过了红绿灯

please turn on the meter   *qǐng dǎbiǎo*   请打表

please give me a receipt *qǐng gěiwǒ kāi fāpiào* 请给我开发票

this is not the right place *búshì zhèlǐ* 不是这里

slow down *qǐng kāi màn yì diǎn* 请开慢一点

People and Family Members

mother *māma* 妈妈

father *bàba* 爸爸

parents *fùmǔ* 父母

family *jiātíng* 家庭

husband *zhàngfu* 丈夫

wife *qīzi* 妻子

children *háizi* 孩子

baby *yīngér* 婴儿

daughter *nǔér* 女儿

son *érzi* 儿子

friend *péngyǒu* 朋友

boyfriend *nán péngyǒu* 男朋友

girlfriend *nǔ péngyǒu* 女朋友

uncle *shūshu* 叔叔

aunt *āyí* 阿姨

grandmother (maternal) *wàipó* 外婆

grandfather (maternal) *wàigōng* 外公

grandmother (paternal) *nǎinai* 奶奶

grandfather (paternal) *yéye* 爷爷

senior *lǎo rén* 老人

Common Adjectives

For a list of the most common Chinese adjective, go to Chapter 2.

Demonstratives

this *zhège* 这个

that *nàge* 那个

these *zhèxie* 这些

those *nàxie* 那些

Common Verbs

Remember, you don't need to conjugate Chinese verbs. Their form remains the same with different speakers and throughout different tenses.

to be   *shì*   是

to buy   *mǎi*   买

to go   *qù*   去

to have   *yǒu*   有

to hear, to listen   *tīng*   听

to like   *xǐ huān*   喜欢

to love   *ài*   爱

to need   *xū yào*   需要

to say, to speak   *shuō*   说

to sell   *mài*   卖

to see, to read   *kàn*   看

to think   *xiǎng*   想

to walk, to go   *zǒu*   走

to want   *yào*   要

Common Places

airport　*jīchǎng*　机场

main train station　*huǒchē zǒngzhàn*　火车总站

embassy　*dàshǐ guǎn*　大使馆

hotel　*jiǔdiàn*　酒店

hostel　*qīngnián sùshè*　青年宿舍

city hall　*shìzhèng fǔ*　市政府

shopping mall　*gòuwù zhōngxīn*　购物中心

restaurant　*fàndiàn*　饭店

fast food restaurant　*kuàicāntīng*　快餐厅

bakery　*miànbāo fáng*　面包房

café　*kāfēi tīng*　咖啡厅

supermarket　*chāoshì*　超市

convenient store　*biànlì diàn*　便利店

pharmacy　*yào fáng*　药房

museum　*bówù guǎn*　博物馆

art gallery　*měishù guǎn*　美术馆

Chapter 4: Numbers, Time and Day

Numbers

0   *líng*   零

1   *yī*   一

2   *èr*   二 (when describing quantities, èr 二 changes to liǎng 两)

3   *sān*   三

4   *sì*   四

5   *wǔ*   五

6   *liù*   六

7   *qī*   七

8   *bā*   八

9   *jiǔ*   九

10   *shí*   十

11   *shí yī*   十一

12   *shí èr*   十二

13   *shí sān*   十三

14   *shí sì*   十四

15   *shí wǔ*   十五

16	*shí liù*	十六
17	*shí qī*	十七
18	*shí bā*	十八
19	*shí jiǔ*	十九
20	*èr shí*	二十
21	*èr shí yī*	二十一
22	*èr shí èr*	二十二
30	*sān shí*	三十
40	*sì shí*	四十
50	*wǔ shí*	五十
60	*liù shí*	六十
70	*qī shí*	七十
80	*bā shí*	八十
90	*jiǔ shí*	九十
100	*yī bǎi*	一百
101	*yī bǎi líng yī*	一百零一
110	*yī bǎi yī shí*	一百一十
111	*yī bǎi yī shí yī*	一百一十一
200	*èr bǎ*	二百 or *liǎng bǎi* 两百
1000	*yī qiān*	一千

10,000   *yī wàn*   一万   (The 10,000, or "wàn" is a unit in Chinese. You'll likely hear larger numbers referred in terms of "wan")

1,000,000 (1 million)   *yī bǎiwàn*   一百万

100,000,000   *yīyì*   一亿   (The 100,000,000 or "yì" is another unit Chinese.)

Numbers Construction – Examples

30
3 + 10 = 30
three [sān 三] + ten[shí 十] =thirty [sānshí 三十]

300
3 + 100 = 300
three [sān 三] + hundred[bǎi 百]=three hundred [sān bǎi 三百]

506
500 + "zero" + 6 = 506
five hundred [wǔ bǎi 五百] + '0' [líng 零]+ six [liù 六] = 506 [wǔ bǎi ling liù 五百零六]
Note that for any "0" gaps in larger numbers, the gap is filled with "ling", or 0.

Counting

Construction: Number + Classifier + Noun

Examples.

one cow   *yì tóu niú*   一头牛
two rabbits   *liǎng zhī tù zi*   两只兔子

Ordinal Numbers

first   dì yī   第一

… first place   dì yī míng   第一名

second   *dì èr*   第二

third   *dì sān*   第三

fourth   *dì sì*   第四

fifth   *dì wǔ*   第五

sixth   *dì liù*   第六

seventh   *dì qī*   第七

eighth   *dì bā*   第八

ninth   *dì jiǔ*   第九

tenth   *dì shí*   第十

eleventh   *dì shí yī*   第十一

twentieth   *dì shí èr*   第十二

50th   *dì wǔ shí*   第五十

100th   *dì yī bǎi*   第一百

Time and Day

<u>Telling Time</u>

What time is it?   *jǐ dian le*   几点了

May I have the time please?   *qǐng wen jǐ dian le*   请问
几点了

O'clock   *dian*   点

Half (30 minutes, for telling time only)   *bàn*   半

Minute   *fēnzhōng*   分钟

Quarter (15 minutes)   *yī kè*   一刻

Note on telling time: The AM/PM concept is not adopted in China. Thus, to indicate the time with respect to the time of day, you can use a time-specific indicator (such as morning, noon, afternoon, evening, midnight).

midnight through early morning　　*língchén*　　凌晨

noon　　*zhōngwǔ*　　中午

morning　　*zǎoshàng*　　早上

afternoon　　*xiàwǔ*　　下午

evening　　*wǎnshàng*　　晚上

Construction: time of day (i.e. afternoon) + hour (i.e. 5) + o'clock [dǐan 点] + minutes (i.e. 35) + min [fēn 分]

Examples.

5:00 AM　　*zǎoshàng wǔ dǐan*　　早上 5 点
5:35 PM　　*xiàwǔ wǔ dǐan sān shí wǔ*　　下午 5 点三十五
12:15 AM　　*língchén shí èr dǐan yī kè*　　凌晨 12 点一刻

Talking about Days

day　　*tiān*　　天

day (used for calendar days)　　*rì*　　日

week　　*xīngqī*　　星期

month　　*yùe*　　月

year *nián* 年

today *jīntiān* 今天

yesterday *zuótiān* 昨天

day before yesterday *qiántiān* 前天

tomorrow *míngtiān* 明天

day after tomorrow *hòutiān* 后天

everyday *měi tiān* 每天

every week *měi xīngqī* 每星期

every month *měi yùe* 每月

this week *zhè ge xīngqī* 这个星期

last week shàng ge xīngqī 上个星期

next week *xià ge xīngqī* 下个星期

holiday *jié rì* 节日

vacation *jià rì* 假日

Chinese New Year chūn jié 春节

Literally, Chinese New Year means "Spring Festival or Spring Holiday."

spring *chūn tiān* 春天

summer *xià tiān* 夏天

fall/autumn *qiū tiān* 秋天

winter   *dōng tiān*   冬天

seasons   *jì jié*   季节

Days of the Week

Monday   *xīngqī yī*   星期一

Tuesday   *xīngqī èr*   星期二

Wednesday   *xīngqī sān*   星期三

Thursday   *xīngqī sì*   星期四

Friday   *xīngqī wǔ*   星期五

Saturday   *xīngqī liù*   星期六

Sunday   *xīngqī tiān*   星期天 or *xīngqī rì*   星期日

Months

Construction: Number of month (i.e. 1 for January) + Month (yuè 月)

January   *yī yuè*   一月

February   *èr yuè*   二月

March   *sān yuè*   三月

April   *sì yuè*   四月

May   *wǔ yuè*   五月

June   *liù yuè*   六月

July   *qī yuè*   七月

August   *bā yuè*   八月

September   *jiǔ yuè*   九月

October   *shí yuè*   十月

November   *shí yī yuè*   十一月

December   *shí èr yuè*   十二月

Writing and saying the date in Chinese is pretty straightforward. Follow the construction below.

Month + Date + [rì 日] + Year + [nián 年]

Example.

November 12, 2015

November *shí yī yùe* + **12** *shí èr* + *rì* + **2015** *èr líng yī wǔ* + *nián*
11 月 12 日 2015 年

65

Chapter 5: Phrases for Specific Situations

Getting to Know Someone

What's your name? *nǐjiào shénme míngzi?* 你叫什么名字?

My name is … *wǒ jiào …* 我叫…

Nice to meet you *hěn gāoxìng rènshì nǐ* 很高兴认识你

Do you speak English? *nǐ huì shuō yīngyǔ ma?* 你会说英语吗?

I can't speak Chinese *wǒ bú huì jiǎng zhōngwén* 我不会讲中文

I speak a little Chinese *wǒ huì shuō yìdiǎn zhōngwén* 我会说一点中文

What language do you speak? *nǐ huì shuō shénme yǔyán* 你会说什么语言

    English *yīngyǔ* 英语

    French *fǎyǔ* 法语

    German *déyǔ* 德语

Spanish   *xībānyáyǔ*   西班牙语

Russian   *é yǔ*   俄语

Italian   *yìdàlìyǔ*   意大利语

Where are you from?   *nǐ shì nǎ lǐ de rén*?   你是哪里的人?

I am from …   *wǒ lái zì*   我来自…

United States of America   *měiguó*   美国

Canada   *jiānádà*   加拿大

England   *yīngguó*   英国

Australia   *àodàliyà*   澳大利亚

China   *zhōngguó*   中国

France   *fǎguó*   法国

Germany   *déguó*   德国

Spain   *xībānyá*   西班牙

New Zealand   *xīnxīlán*   新西兰

Ireland   *àiěrlán*   爱尔兰

Italy   *yìdàlì*   意大利

Russia   *é guó*   俄国

What do you do? *nǐ shì zuò shénme de?* 你是做什么的?

I am a... *wǒ shì...* 我是...

Student *xuéshēng* 学生

Teacher *lǎoshī* 老师

Accountant *kuàijì* 会计

Actor/Actress *yǎnyuán* 演员

Businessman/ Businesswoman *shāngrén* 商人

Chef *chúshī* 厨师

Computer Engineer *diànnǎo gōngchéngshī* 电脑工程师

Dentist *yákē yīshēng* 牙科医生

Designer *shèjìshī* 设计师

Doctor *yīshēng* 医生

Engineer *gōngchéngshī* 工程师

Entrepreneur *chuàngyèjiā* 创业家

Journalist *jìzhě* 记者

Lawyer *lǜ shī* 律师

Musician *yīnyuè jiā* 音乐家

Nurse *hùshì* 护士

Secretary *mìshū* 秘书

Writer *zuò jiā* 作家

Retired *tuìxiū* 退休

Have you been to China before? *nǐ yǐqián láiguò zhōngguó ma?* 你以前来过中国吗？

What do you like to do? *nǐ xǐhuān zuò shénme?* 你喜欢做什么？

I like to travel *wǒ xǐhuān qù lǚyóu* 我喜去欢旅游

Eating Out

meal *cān* 餐

breakfast *zǎocān* 早餐

lunch *wǔcān* 午餐

afternoon tea *xiàwǔ chá* 下午茶

dinner *wǎncān* 晚餐

food *fàn* 饭

snack (i.e. chips, cookies) *língshí* 零食

snack (i.e. street food, finger food, a light meal) *xiǎo chī* 小吃

Have you eaten? *nǐ chīfàn le ma?* 你吃饭了吗?

I'm hungry *wǒ è le* 我饿了

Let's go eat *wǒmen qù chīfàn ba* 我们去吃饭吧

Ordering Food

How many people? *jǐ wèi* 几位?

    1 person *yí wèi* 一位

    2 people *liǎng wèi* 两位

    3 people *sān wèi* 三位

    4 people *sì wèi* 四位

    5 people *wǔ wèi* 五位

    6 people *liù wèi* 六位

    10 people *shí wèi* 七位

menu *càidān* 菜单

Can I look at the menu, please? *qǐng gěi wǒ kànkan càidān* 请给我看看菜单

Do you have an English menu? *nǐ yǒu méi yǒu yīngwén càidān?* 你有没有英文菜单?

> **Yes, we have one** *yǒu* 有
>
> **No, we don't have one** *méi yǒu* 没有

I'm a vegetarian *wǒ chī sù* 我吃素

Is this (menu item) vegetarian? *zhège shì sù de ma?* 这个是素的吗?

Do you have vegetarian dishes? *nǐmen yǒu sù shí ma?* 你们有素食吗?

I'm allergic to … *wǒ dùi* (insert allergen name) *guòmǐn* 我对___过敏

> **eggs** *jīdàn* 鸡蛋
>
> **fish** *yú* 鱼
>
> **dairy** *nǎi lèi* 奶类
>
> **nuts** *jiān guǒ* 坚果
>
> **peanuts** *huāshēng* 花生
>
> **shellfish** (incl. Shrimp) *bèiké lèi* 贝壳类
>
> **shrimp** *xiā* 虾

soy (products) *huángdòu lèi* 黄豆类

wheat/gluten (products) *màilèi shípǐn* 麦类食品

Does this contain… ? *zhège hányǒu* (insert allergen name) *ma?* 这个含有 … 吗?

Can you recommend me some specialty dishes? *kéyǐ tūijiàn yìxiē tèsè cài ma?* 可以推荐一些特色菜吗?

Is this spicy? *zhège shì là de ma?* 这个是辣的吗?

I don't want it spicy *wǒ búyào là de* 我不要辣的

mild spicy *shǎo là* 少辣

Is it warm? *zhège shì rè de ma?* 这个是热的吗？

cold *liáng de* 凉的

I don't want ice *wǒ búyào bīng* 我不要冰

less/easy ice *shǎo bīng* 少冰

Asking for Service

waiter/waitress *fúwù yuán* 服务员

sir *xiānshēng* 先生

miss xiǎojiě 小姐

Local restaurant eaters refer to the waiter as "handsome guy" [shuài gē 帅哥] and the waitress as "beautiful lady" [měi nǚ 美女].

please get me ...   *qǐng bāng wǒ ná ...*   请帮我拿 ...

    a fork   *yī bǎ chāzi*   一把叉子

    a knife   *yī bǎ cāndāo*   一把餐刀

    a spoon   *yī bǎ sháozi*   一把勺子

    a bowl   *yī ge wǎn*   一个碗

    a plate   *yī ge pánzi*   一个盘子

    a glass   *cup yī ge bēizi*   一个杯子

    a pair of chopsticks   *yī shuāng kuàizi*   一双筷子

    some napkin   *cānjīn zhǐ*   餐巾纸

Please bring me the menu again   *qǐng zài gěiwǒ kàn yíxià càidān*   请再给我看一下菜单

This .... is dirty   *zhè ge ... shì zāng de*   这个...   是脏的

Please bring me another one   *qǐng bāng wǒ zài ná yí ge*
请帮我再拿一个

Food

meat   *ròu*   肉

beef   *niúròu*   牛肉

pork   *zhūròu*   猪肉

lamb   *yángròu*   羊肉

chicken   *jīròu*   鸡肉

fish   *yú*   鱼

seafood   *hǎixiān*   海鲜

cheese   *nǎilào*   奶酪

eggs   *jīdàn*   鸡蛋

bread   *miànbāo*   面包

noodles   *miàntiáo*   面条

rice   *mǐfàn*   米饭

fried rice   *chǎofàn*   炒饭

dumpling   *jiǎozi*   饺子

sauce   *jiàng*   酱

sweet and sour   *tiánsuān*   甜酸

barbecue   *shāokǎo*   烧烤

sandwich   *sānmíngzhì*   三明治

hamburger *hànbǎobāo* 汉堡包

pizza *bǐsà* 比萨

fries *shǔtiáo* 薯条

ketchup *fānqiéjiàng* 番茄酱

mayonnaise *měinǎizī* 美乃滋

Beverages

coffee shop *kāfēi tīng* 咖啡厅

coffee *kāfēi* 咖啡

black coffee *hēi kāfēi* 黑咖啡

(café) latte *ná tiě* 拿铁

cappuccino *kǎ bù qí nuò* 卡布奇诺

espresso *nóngsuō kāfēi* 浓缩咖啡

macchiato *mǎ qí duǒ* 玛奇朵

Americano *měi shì kāfēi* 美式咖啡

creamer *nǎijīng* 奶精

milk *niúnǎi* 牛奶

soy milk *dòu nǎi* 豆奶

almond milk *xìngrén nǎi* 杏仁奶

sugar *táng* 糖

sugar free sweetener *wú táng tiánwèi jì* 无糖甜味剂

tea *chá* 茶

green tea *lùchá* 绿茶

scented tea *huāchá* 花茶

black tea *hóngchá* 红茶

juice *guǒzhī* 果汁

water *shuǐ* 水

mineral water *kuàngquán shuǐ* 矿泉水

beer *píjiǔ* 啤酒

red wine *hóng pútáo jiǔ* 红葡萄酒

white wine *bái pútáo jiǔ* 白葡萄酒

Ordering Food

I/we want (one)…. *yào (yī ge)...* 要一个

Examples.

one kung pao chicken *yī ge gōngbào jīdīng* 一个宫爆
鸡丁

one broccoli beef   *yī ge jièlán niúròu*   两个芥兰牛肉

two spicy garlic eggplant   *liǎng ge yúxiāng qiézi*   两个鱼香茄子

one (glass of) beer   *yī bēi píjiǔ*   一杯啤酒

two (glasses of) beers   *liǎng bēi píjiǔ*   两杯啤酒

For more on ordering alcoholic drinks, see the section, At the Bar.

one bowl of rice   *yī wǎn mǐfàn*   碗米饭

three bowls of rice   *sān wǎn mǐfàn*   三碗米饭

Asking for the Check

check please   *mǎidān*   买单

I don't need change   *búyòng zhǎo qián*   不用找钱

Can I pay with a card?   *kěyǐ shuākǎ ma?*   可以刷卡吗?

It's delicious   *hěn hǎochī*   很好吃

Note, in China and Taiwan, it's not expected of customers to leave a tip after eating.

Shopping and Bargaining

<u>Bargaining</u>

How much is this?　　*zhège duōshǎo qián?*　　这个多少钱？

700 RMB　　*qībǎi yuán* (or *qībǎi kuài*)　　七百元（七百块）

too expensive　　*tài guì le*　　太贵了

Would you take (this amount)?　　(insert amount) *yuán kěyǐ ma?*　　__元可以吗？

expensive　　*guì*　　贵

cheap　　*piányi*　　便宜

Can you sell it for cheaper?　　*kěyǐ zài piányì diǎn ma?*　可以再便宜点吗？

I can't afford it/ I didn't bring enough money　　*wǒ dài de qián búgòu*　　我带的钱不够

I don't want it　　*wǒ bù yào*　　我不要

I'm not interested　　*wǒ méiyǒu xìngqù*　　我没有兴趣

You're cheating me   *nǐ piàn wǒ*   你骗我

I'll take it (this)   *wǒ yào mǎi zhège*   我要买这个

Choosing a Color

I want it in (color)...   *wǒ yào* (insert color) *de*   我要...的

Do you have it in (color)…   *yǒu méi yǒu* (insert color) *de*   有没有...的

black   *hēi sè*   黑色

white   *bái sè*   白色

grey   *huī sè*   灰色

red   *hóng sè*   红色

blue   *lán sè*   蓝色

yellow   *huáng sè*   黄色

green   *lǜ sè*   绿色

orange   *chéng sè*   橙色

purple   *zǐ sè*   紫色

brown   *zōng sè*   棕色

gold   *jīn sè*   金色

silver *yín sè* 银色

Asking for Sizes

Do you have this in my size? *yǒu méi yǒu wǒde chǐcùn*
有没有我的尺寸

Do you have this in (size)? *yǒu méi yǒu* (insert size) *hào de*? 有没有... 号的?

    small *xiǎo* 小

    medium *zhōng* 中

    large *dà* 大

    X-large *chāo dà* 超大

too big *tài dà le* 太大了

too small *tài xiǎo le* 太小了

Payment and Shipping

to pay *fù qián* 付钱

cash *xiàn jīn* 现金

Do you take credit card? *shōu xìn yòng kǎ ma?* 收信用卡吗?

Please give a receipt   *qǐng gěi wǒ gè fāpiào*   请给我个发票

Please give me change   *qǐng zhǎo qián*   请找钱

Please give me a bag   *qǐng gěi wǒ ge dàizi*   请给我个袋子

Do you ship (overseas)?   *kěyǐ jì dào hǎiwài ma?*   可以寄到海外吗？

Can you ship/send it to my hotel?   *kěyǐ sòng dào wǒde jiǔdiàn ma?*   可以送到我的酒店吗?

This is the address   *zhè shì dìzhǐ*   这是地址

Money and Currency

Currency

RMB (renminbi)   *rén mín bì*   人民币   (RMB 'rén mín bì' literally means people's money)

NTD (New Taiwan Dollar)   *xīn tái bì*   新台币

Hong Kong Dollar   *gǎng bì*   港币

U.S. Dollar   *měi yuán*   美元

Euro *ōu yuán* 欧元

Pound *yīng bàng* 英镑

Australian Dollar *ào yuán* 澳元

Canadian Dollar *jiā bì* 加币

Banking and Exchanging Money

bank *yín háng* 银行

exchange money *huàn qián* 换钱

Where can I exchange money (please)? *qǐngwèn, zài nǎli kěyi huàn qián?* 请问在哪里可以换钱?

I want to exchange (500) U.S. dollars *wǒ yào huàn (wǒ bǎi) měiyuán* 我要换 500 美元

What is the exchange rate? *huì lü shì shénme?* 汇率是什么?

cash *xiàn jīn* 现金

check *zhī piào* 支票

I want to withdraw money *wǒ yào tí kuǎn* 我要提款

traveler's check *lü xíng zhī piào* 旅行支票

credit card *xìn yòng kǎ* 信用卡

password/pin number *mì mǎ* 密码

passport *hù zhào* 护照

ID card *shēn fèn zhèng* 身份证

visa *qiān zhèng* 签证

At the Bar

Do you serve alcohol? *mài búmài jiǔ?* 卖不卖酒？

Is there table service? *yǒu méiyǒu cānzhuō fúwù?* 有没有餐桌服务？

cheers *gānbēi* 干杯

Types of Drinks

draft (draught) beer *zhāpí* 扎啤

red wine *hóng pútáojiǔ* 红葡萄酒

white wine *bái pútáojiǔ* 白葡萄酒

champagne *xiāng bīn* 香槟

whiskey *wēi shì jì* 威士忌

vodka *fú tè jiā* 伏特加

rum   *lán mǔ jiǔ*   兰姆酒

gin   *dù song zǐ jiǔ*   杜松子酒酒

tequila   *lóng shé lán jiǔ*   龙舌兰酒

cocktail   *jīwěi jiǔ*   鸡尾酒

gin and tonic   *jīn tāng lì*   金汤力

soda water/ club soda   *sūdǎ shuǐ*   苏打水

tonic water   *tōngníng shuǐ*   通宁水

orange juice   *chéngzhī*   橙汁

coca cola   *kělè*   可乐

sprite   *xuěbì*   雪碧

Ordering Drinks

a glass of something...
Number + Classifier for glass (*bēi*) + Beverage name

a bottle of something...
Number + Classifier for bottle (*píng*) + Beverage name

mixed drinks...
Hard liquor (i.e. rum) + add (*jiā*)+ Mixer (i.e. coke)

Examples.

a glass of beer, please   *qǐng gěiwǒ yībēi píjiǔ*   请给我一杯啤酒

a glass of red wine, please   *qǐng gěiwǒ yībēi hóng pútáojiǔ* 请给我一杯红葡萄酒

a bottle of beer, please   *qǐng gěi wǒ yīpíng píjiǔ*   请给我一瓶啤酒

jack and coke   *wēi shì jì jiā kělè*   威士忌加可乐

rum and coke   *lán mǔ jiǔ jiā kělè*   郎姆酒加可乐

Do you have any bar snacks?   *yǒu méi yǒu chī de?* 有没有吃的？

one more, please   *qǐng zài gěi wǒ yī gè*   请再给我一个

one more round, please   *qǐng zài lái yī lún*   请再来一轮

That's enough   *gòu le*   够了

I'm a bit drunk   *wo yǒu diǎn zùi le*   我有点醉了

What is the closing time?   *jǐdiǎn guān mén?*   几点关门？

Romantic Endeavors

I like you   *wǒ xǐhuan nǐ*   我喜欢你

I love you   *wǒ ài nǐ*   我爱你

I miss you   *wǒ xiǎng nǐ*   我想你

Do you have a boyfriend?   *nǐ yǒu nán péngyǒu ma?*   你有男朋友吗?

I have a boyfriend   *wǒ yǒu nán péngyǒu*   我有男朋友

I don't have a boyfriend   *wǒ méi yǒu nán péngyǒu*   我没有男朋友

Do you have a girlfriend?   *nǐ yǒu nǚ péngyǒu ma?*   你有女朋友吗?

I don't have a girlfriend   *wǒ méi yǒu nǚ péngyǒu*   我没有女朋友

Are you here alone?   *yígè rén ma?*   一个人吗?

May I sit here?   *wǒ kěyǐ zuò zhè er ma?*   我可以坐这儿吗?

May I have your name?   *kěyǐ gàosù wǒ nǐde míngzi ma?*   可以告诉我你的名字吗?

Would you like to dance with me? *kěyǐ qǐng nǐ tiàowǔ ma?* 可以请你跳舞吗？

May I buy you a drink? *kěyǐ qǐng nǐ hē yì bēi ma?* 可以请你喝一杯吗？

Do you live nearby? *nǐ zhù zài fùjìn ma?* 你住在附近吗？

Let's take a walk outside *chūqù zǒuzou zěnme yàng?* 出去走走怎么样？

May I have your phone number? *kěyǐ liúxia nǐde diànhuà hàomǎ ma?* 可以留下你的电话号码吗？

May I call you? *kěyǐ gěi nǐ dǎ diànhuà ma?* 可以给你打电话吗？

Complimenting Someone

You have a lovely smile! *nǐ xiào qǐlai hěn hǎokàn* 你笑起来很好看

You are funny (you've a funny personality) *nǐ hěn fēngqù* 你很风趣

You are really special *nǐ hěn tèbié* 你很特别

You are beautiful   *nǐ hěn měi*   你很美

You are handsome   *nǐ hěn shuài*   你很帅

You are really sexy   *nǐ zhēn xìnggǎn*   你真性感

You have a beautiful name   *nǐ de míngzi zhēn hǎotīng*

你的名字真好听

Chapter 6: Recognize the Most Useful Chinese Characters

Men's/ Women's Restroom

Male nán 男

Female nǚ 女

Turn On/ Off Appliances

On (literally open) kāi 开

Off (literally close) guān 关

Up/ Down

Up shàng 上

Down xià 下

Going in and out - Entrance and Exit

Entrance (in) rù kǒu 入口

Exit (out) chū kǒu 出口

Push/ Pull

Push tūi 推

Pull lā 拉

Warning Signs

Forbidden jìnzhǐ 禁止

Dangerous wēixiǎn 危险

Watch Out/ Be Careful dāngxīn 当心

Written Numbers

1 yī 一

2 èr 二

3 sān 三

4 sì 四

5 wǔ 五

6 liù 六

7 qī 七

8 bā 八

9 jiǔ 九

10 shí 十

Reference Information

Pronunciation Guide

Tone	First	Second	Third	Fourth	Fifth
Pinyin	ā	á	ǎ	à	a
Description	High	Rising	Low or dipping	Falling	Neutral, light
Example	mā	má	mǎ	mà	ma

Initial Sounds: Exactly Like English

f　father

l　love

m　mom

n　no

s　sing

sh　ship, shank

w　way

y　yes

Initial Sounds: Slightly Different from English

This list is, for the most part, similar to their English counterparts. Pay attention to the nuanced differences.

b   b**ud**, **b**u**bb**le

ch   **ch**ap, dit**ch**

d   **c**ig, ma**d**

g   **g**oat, ci**g**ar

h   **h**en, **h**a**h**a

j   **g**enie, **j**eep

k   **k**en

p   **p**op

t   **t**ip

z   **z**en, **z**est

Initial Sounds: Tricky and Really Different From English

Pay close attention to this list.

c   **ts**ar (cong = ts-ong)

q   **ch**eese, **ch**eat (qin = chin)

r   **r**ut, **r**uth (re = r'ugh)

94

x   **shee**p (xi = shee)

zh   **g**em, **j**ob, **j**ack (zhang = jahng)

Simple Vowels

a   **fa**ther

e   sound in between "**eh**" and "**uh**"

i   **i**s, w**e**

o   **aw**, **a**ll, w**o**e

u   w**oo**, s**ou**p

ü   **yooo**

Compound Finals	Nasal Ending Finals	
ai **eye**, b**ye**	*an* **an**	*ang* **ahng, hung**
ao h**ow**	*en* h**en**	*eng* **uhng**
ei h**ey**	*ian* kardash**ian**	*iang* **eon**
ia **-ya**, ma**ya**	*in* **in**	*ing* **-ying**, say**ing**
iao **-yao (ee-auw)**	*uan* **woo-an**	*iong* **ee-own**

95

ie **ee-yeh**	*üan* **yoo-an**	*ong* **ohng**
iou **ee-owe**	*uen* **woo-en**	*uang* **woo-ahng**
ou **owe**	*ün* **yoon**	*ueng* **woo-ehng**
ua **wooah**		
uai **wooeye**		
üe **yoo-eh**		
uei **woo-aey**		
uo **woo-woh**		

Pronunciation Audio Link

Pronunciation Chart for every initial sound and vowel combination:

https://chinese.yabla.com/chinese-pinyin-chart.php

Stay Connected

Your Feedback Is Valuable To Me

Dear readers, I would really appreciate it if you could send any feedback to polyglotlanguageguides@gmail.com. I will take time to review each comment and incorporate your feedback into my next edition.

Conclusion

Thank you for reading and purchasing this guidebook. I hope you will find it useful on your trip abroad. Learning Chinese for the first time may be daunting, but if you break the language down into pieces and focus on the most commonly used phrases and words, the Chinese language becomes very manageable. When you are in the country, do practice with the Chinese locals. In fact, Chinese locals absolutely love it when visitors learn their language and often voluntarily exchange conversations with travelers.

I hope you enjoyed my guidebook and I would really appreciate it if you could take two minutes to leave a review.

谢谢 Xiè xiè!

Celine Li
Polyglot Language Guides

27549680R00058

Made in the USA
San Bernardino, CA
14 December 2015